Five reasons why you'll love Isadora Moon . . .

Meet the magical, fangtastic Isadora Moon!

Isadora is half vampire, half fairy, totally unique!

You'll love her spellbinding winter activities!

Discover the magical ice palace!

Enchanting pink and black pictures

OXFORD
UNIVERSITY PRESS

Great Clarendon Street, Oxford OX2 6DP

Oxford University Press is a department of the University of Oxford.
It furthers the University's objective of excellence in research, scholarship,
and education by publishing worldwide. Oxford is a registered trade mark
of Oxford University Press in the UK and in certain other countries

Copyright © Harriet Muncaster 2020 and 2022

The moral rights of the author have been asserted

Database right Oxford University Press (maker)

First published by PENGUIN RANDOM HOUSE GRUPO EDITORIAL,
Spain, as Diversión y juegos con Isadora Moon in 2020

This edition first published by Oxford University Press in 2022

All rights reserved. No part of this publication may be reproduced,
stored in a retrieval system, or transmitted, in any form or by any means,
without the prior permission in writing of Oxford University Press,
or as expressly permitted by law, or under terms agreed with the appropriate
reprographics rights organization. Enquiries concerning reproduction
outside the scope of the above should be sent to the Rights Department,
Oxford University Press, at the address above

You must not circulate this book in any other binding or cover
and you must impose this same condition on any acquirer

British Library Cataloguing in Publication Data

Data available

ISBN: 978-0-19-278582-4

1 3 5 7 9 10 8 6 4 2

Printed in Great Britain by Bell and Bain Ltd, Glasgow

Paper used in the production of this book is a natural,
recyclable product made from wood grown in sustainable forests.
The manufacturing process conforms to the environmental
regulations of the country of origin.

MIX
Paper from
responsible sources
FSC
www.fsc.org
FSC® C007785

The Winter Magic
Activity Book

Harriet Muncaster

OXFORD
UNIVERSITY PRESS

Sleepover

A chilly winter's night is the perfect time for a sleepover.
Colour in the drawing and add your own magical details to
help Isadora feel at home in Zoe's house.

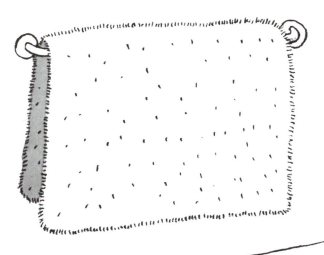

Look and Find

- ★ Two pink bottles
- ★ A toy dinosaur
- ★ Eleven stars
- ★ A bat-shaped pen
- ★ Two drawing pins
- ★ A boy without a tie
- ★ Three pairs of scissors
- ★ Three stamps

Mysterious Castle

Isadora found lots of interesting things when she visited a castle. Can you find them in the word search?

```
R L A C S R C W Q J H L
D Y V R N A U U I U D X
C G H O S T N O Z L X D
A Y A W F E Z P E V B O
W B D N S T A I N C Y G
Y G U H C Y H K G R I S
U H R J B S U J B W R P
F K A N E S O X R A T J
A S Q T L S E W T S C A
K C R F L N T A S M P N
L Q W A R M O U R B E T
```

Crown

Shield

Ghost

Armour

Ballet Show

Isadora loves the ballet and practises every day!
She has come to watch a show starring her favourite dancer,
Tatiana Tutu. Draw a ballet scene on the stage.

Vampire Sudoku

Can you help Isadora and her friends solve this
sudoku puzzle? Each row, column, and rectangle
needs to include numbers 1 to 6.

		3		1	
5	6		3	2	
	5	4	2		3
2		6	4	5	
	1	2		4	5
	4			3	2

What's Next?

Can you work out what comes next in the series?
Draw your answers in the boxes.

Magical Mix-Up

There has been a mix-up with the presents!
Follow the wriggly lines to find out who each one belongs to!

Carrot

Book
of spells

Ballet shoes

Mysterious Meal

Someone has been casting magical spells at the table!
There are seven differences between the two pictures.
Can you find them all?

Favourite Things

Unscramble the letters in each box to find out what
Pink Rabbit's favourite things are.

KOBSO

- -

NCDANIG

- -

AKEC

- -

STPENSRE

- -

TAE

- -

IARASDO

- -

Star Gazing

Isadora's dad, Count Bartholomew Moon, loves looking at the stars. What shapes or patterns do you think he can see? Use your drawing skills to make your own star patterns here.

What a Mess!

Isadora's magic has gone wrong and she's mixed up summer and winter! Can you sort out the mess by circling the winter drawings?

A New Friend

On a visit to the enchanted castle, Isadora and her friends meet someone new. Join the dots to find out who it is.

Wintry Riddles

As well as magic tricks, Cousin Wilbur knows a lot of riddles! Do you know the answers to these wintry puzzles?

1. I can drift, swirl and fall. There are many of us, but none of us look exactly the same. What I am?

2. I live in lands of snow and ice. I have wings but cannot fly. What am I?

3. I have five fingers but no arms. I'll keep you warm on a frosty day. What am I?

4. I am round but I do not bounce. You will get cold hands if you hold me. What am I?

Tasty Treats

Countess Cordelia Moon has made a delicious cake!
Use your colouring pencils to complete the picture.

Musical Mix-Up

Isadora and her school friends are practising their
instruments. Can you match the words to the pictures?

Tambourine

Flute

Clarinet

Drum

Guitar

Trumpet

Icy Magic

If you could create a magical creature out of snow,
what would it look like? Draw your idea here.

Ice Palace

Isadora and the Snow Boy are exploring the ice palace,
but some things have magically disappeared.
Can you number the missing images?

Magical Friends

Pink Rabbit was a stuffed toy until Isadora's Mum magicked him to life! If you could magic one of your toys to life, what would it be?

I would choose:

....

My toy would be able to do these magical things:

1. ....

2. ....

3. ....

Undersea World

Isadora has magically escaped the cold winter weather to go exploring under the sea! Can you copy the fish onto the grid?

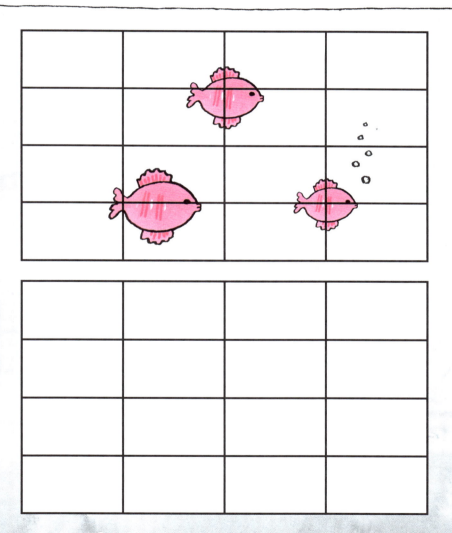

The Perfect Present

Isadora wants to give Zoe a present, but she isn't sure what human children like. Help her pick a present and explain why you have chosen it.

I have chosen a:

....

Because:

....

....

....

A Magical Treat

If you could use magic to give yourself a wintry treat what would it be? Maybe it's a new toy or something delicious to eat? Draw your idea here.

Guess Who I Am

Solve the clues to guess which of the characters in the picture they describe and then write down what you like about them.

I have hands but no feet.

I can breathe underwater.

I love to swim.

The fish are my friends.

The character is:

....

and what I like about them is:

....

....

....

Super Memory

Look very closely at the picture on the next page and then answer these questions. Can you remember everything?

1. How many children are sitting on the sofa?

....

2. What is Pink Rabbit doing?

....

3. How many children are wearing a scarf?

....

4. How many children are wearing shoes?

....

5. What is pictured on the teapot?

....

6. What kind of animals are on the back of the sofa and armchair?

....

7. Where is the magic wand?

....

8. How many plant pots are there?

....

9. How many spoons are on the table?

....

Fancy Dress

Isadora has dressed up as a mermaid.
Can you use the words below to label her costume?

TIARA * MAGIC MIRROR * SCALES *
FINS * SHELLS * PINCERS

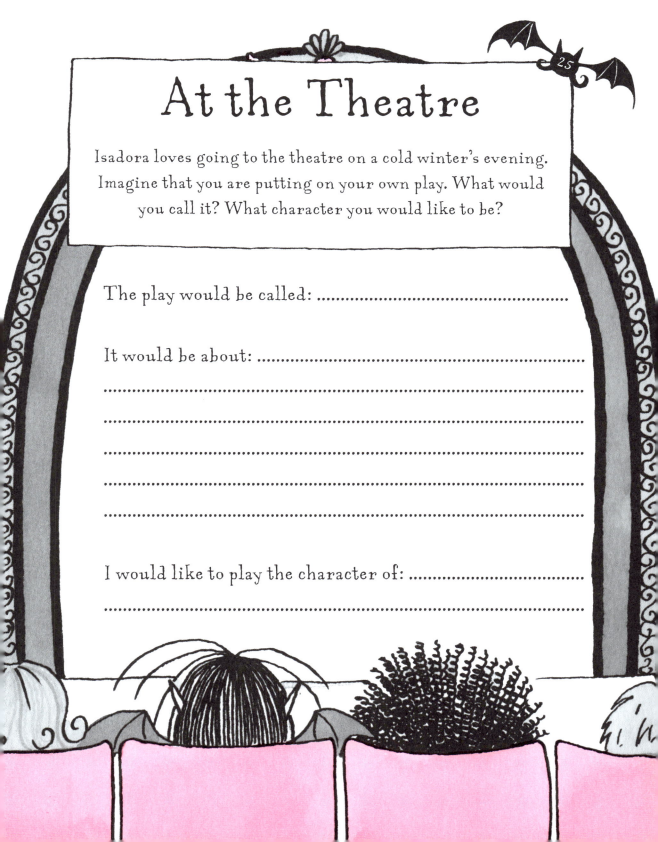

At the Theatre

Isadora loves going to the theatre on a cold winter's evening. Imagine that you are putting on your own play. What would you call it? What character you would like to be?

The play would be called: ....

It would be about: ....

....

....

....

....

I would like to play the character of: ....

....

Perfect Match

Can you match the words below with
the thing they describe?

BOUNCY

SPINNING

HAIRY

SCARY

CROAKING

FUN

JUMPING

MUSICAL

MISCHIEVOUS

Party Time

Isadora and Zoe are making food for a party! How many of each thing do they need? Circle the correct numbers.

3+1 =

3   4   5

3+2 =

4   5   6

4+5 =

8   9   10

Pink Rabbit Needs Help

Pink Rabbit is trapped in a bubble and can't reach the things he's looking for. Can you help him out by finding the objects in the boxes?

What do you see in the grid below?

Square A4..............................

Square B2..............................

Square B5..............................

Square C1..............................

Square D3..............................

Square D4..............................

	1	2	3	4	5
A					
B					
C					
D					

Prize Silhouettes

Isadora and Araminta won the award for the best performance at the show. But which was the winning silhouette? Circle the one you think is correct.

What Is My Name?

Isadora's dad is a vampire, but can you remember his name?
Go through the boxes in number order
to find the answer.

2 THO

6 ON

4 MEW

3 LO

1 BAR

5 MO

Breakfast Time!

Countess Cordelia Moon has made Isadora and Honeyblossom a delicious breakfast. Can you unscramble the letters to find out what they are eating? Use the picture below to help you!

A J M

SARSOCINTS

- - - - - - - - - - - - - - - - - -   - - - - - - - - - - - - - - - - - -

S A T T O

- - - - - - - - - - - - - - - - - -

Ice Path

The Snow Boy is lost! If he doesn't get home before sunrise he'll melt. Can you help him find his way to Isadora before it's too late?

Fairy Garden

Countess Cordelia has cast a magical spell to keep the garden alive over winter. Cross out the flowers and plants that are repeated to find out what has been hidden here.

Fairy School

As a half vampire, Isadora is not very happy about being sent
to fairy school! Can you make it look a little bit more vampire?
Colour in the picture and add your own vampire details.

A Magical Fair

Isadora and her friends had a wonderful time at the fair! Can you find the things they saw there in the wordsearch.

```
R L M C S R C W Q J H L
D Y O R N A U U I U D X
C A N D Y F L O S S X D
A Y S W F E Z P L V B O
W B T O S T A B N J Y G
Y G E H C Y H A G H I S
C A R O U S E L E W R P
F K A N E S O L R K T J
A S Q T L S E O T S C A
K C R F L N T O S B P N
L Q W I R K O N W Z E T
```

Candy Floss

Monster

Balloon

Carousel

Snowy Magic

Aunt Crystal turned Isadora's garden into a winter wonderland. Draw your own snowy garden here. It could be inspired by a real garden or an imaginary one.

Look and Find

- ★ A witch's hat
- ★ A round window
- ★ A wizard's hat
- ★ A ferris wheel
- ★ A wand
- ★ Three lamp posts
- ★ A basket

More Sudoku Fun

Isadora and her friends are doing another sudoku puzzle.
Can you help them to solve it? Each row, column,
and rectangle needs to include numbers 1 to 6.

3			5	2	6
	6	2		1	
2		3	1		4
1	4				2
	2		6	3	
6		5		4	1

What's Next?

Can you work out what comes next in the series?
Draw your answers in the boxes.

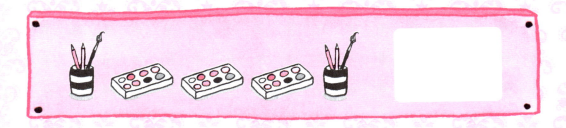

Snow Days

Isadora loves playing in the snow. Unscramble the letters in each box to find out what she needs for a perfect snow day!

ATH

OVELGS

FRASC

ATOC

OBOST

LEEDGS

Holiday Plans

It's almost time for Isadora's school holiday. What are your favourite things to in the holidays when it's cold and wintry? Draw them here!

Dressing-Up Fun!

Isadora's friends are ready for a fancy-dress party.
Can you follow the wriggly lines to match the friends to their
characters' favourite things?

The sea

Fire

Flowers

Magic in Class

There's something strange happening in the classroom!
Can you spot seven differences between the pictures?

In a Muddle!

Isadora needs to choose a gift for her mum, but she's got herself into a muddle. Which objects don't belong here? Circle the three things that look more suited to a vampire than a fairy!

I'm Hungry!

Pink Rabbit has not had his breakfast and is feeling hungry.
Join the dots to find out what he wants to eat.

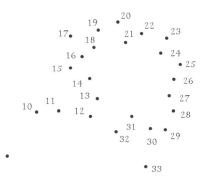

A Gift for Isadora!

Cross out all of the gift boxes that are repeated to find out which present is for Isadora.

A Trip to the Castle

When Isadora and her class visited an old castle, they met Oscar the ghost! Can you imagine who else might live in a castle? Draw a picture here.

Riddle Magic

Half witch Mirabelle has been coming up with magic-themed riddles. Do you know the answers to these spellbinding puzzles?

1. I can fly, but I have no wings. You might see me used for sweeping the floor. What am I?

2. I look like a big pot, but you don't use me to cook dinner. You can use me to make magic potions. What am I?

3. I have wings but I am not a bird. My breath is fiery. What am I?

4. I am black but I'm not a cat. I'm tall and pointy. What am I?

A Tasty Treat

Carrot cake is Pink Rabbit's favourite! Copy the drawing into the grid below and colour it in.

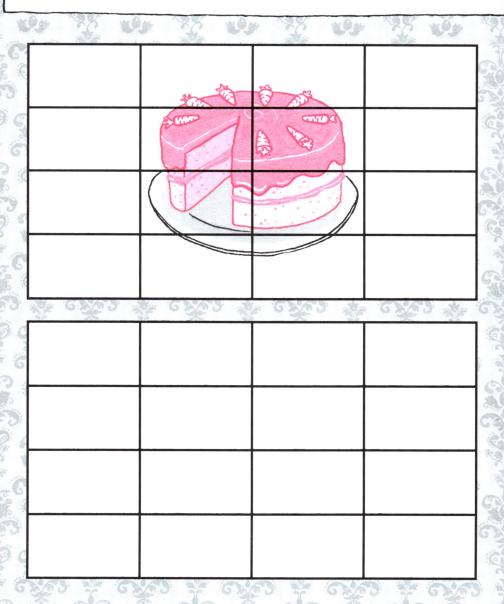

A Surprise Guest

A dragon has snuck into Isadora's bathroom. What a mess! Can you number the missing images?

Answers

Activity 2

Activity 3

Activity 5

4	2	3	5	1	6
5	6	1	3	2	4
1	5	4	2	6	3
2	3	6	4	5	1
3	1	2	6	4	5
6	4	5	1	3	2

Activity 6

Activity 8

Activity 9

BOOKS, DANCING, CAKE, PRESENTS, TEA, ISADORA

Activity 11

Activity 13

1. snowflake, 2. penguin, 3. glove, 4. snowball

Activity 15

Tambourine

Drum

Clarinet

Flute

Guitar

Trumpet

Activity 17

 2

 1

 4

 5

 3

 6

Answers

Activity 22

Princess Delphina, the mermaid

Activity 23

1. 4
2. sleeping
3. 1
4. 0
5. bats
6. bats
7. in a plant pot
8. 3
9. 1

Activity 24

Tiara

Magic Mirror

Shells

Pincers

Scales

Fins

Activity 26

 BOUNCY, CROAKING, JUMPING

 SPINNING, FUN, MUSICAL

 HAIRY, MISCHIEVOUS, SCARY

Activity 27

4, 5, 9

Activity 28

A4: balloon, B2: carton of tomato juice, B5: stars, C1: books, D3: crown, D4: jug of juice

Activity 29

 4

Activity 30

BARTHOLOMEW MOON

Activity 31

JAM, CROISSANTS, TOAST

Activity 32

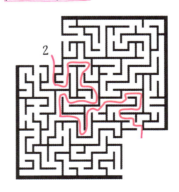

2

Answers

Activity 33

Activity 35

Activity 37

Activity 38

3	1	4	5	2	6
5	6	2	4	1	3
2	5	3	1	6	4
1	4	6	3	5	2
4	2	1	6	3	5
6	3	5	2	4	1

Activity 39

Activity 40

HAT, GLOVES, SCARF, COAT, BOOTS, SLEDGE

Activity 43

Activity 44

Activity 46

Activity 48

1. broom, 2. cauldron, 3. dragon, 4. witch's hat

Activity 50